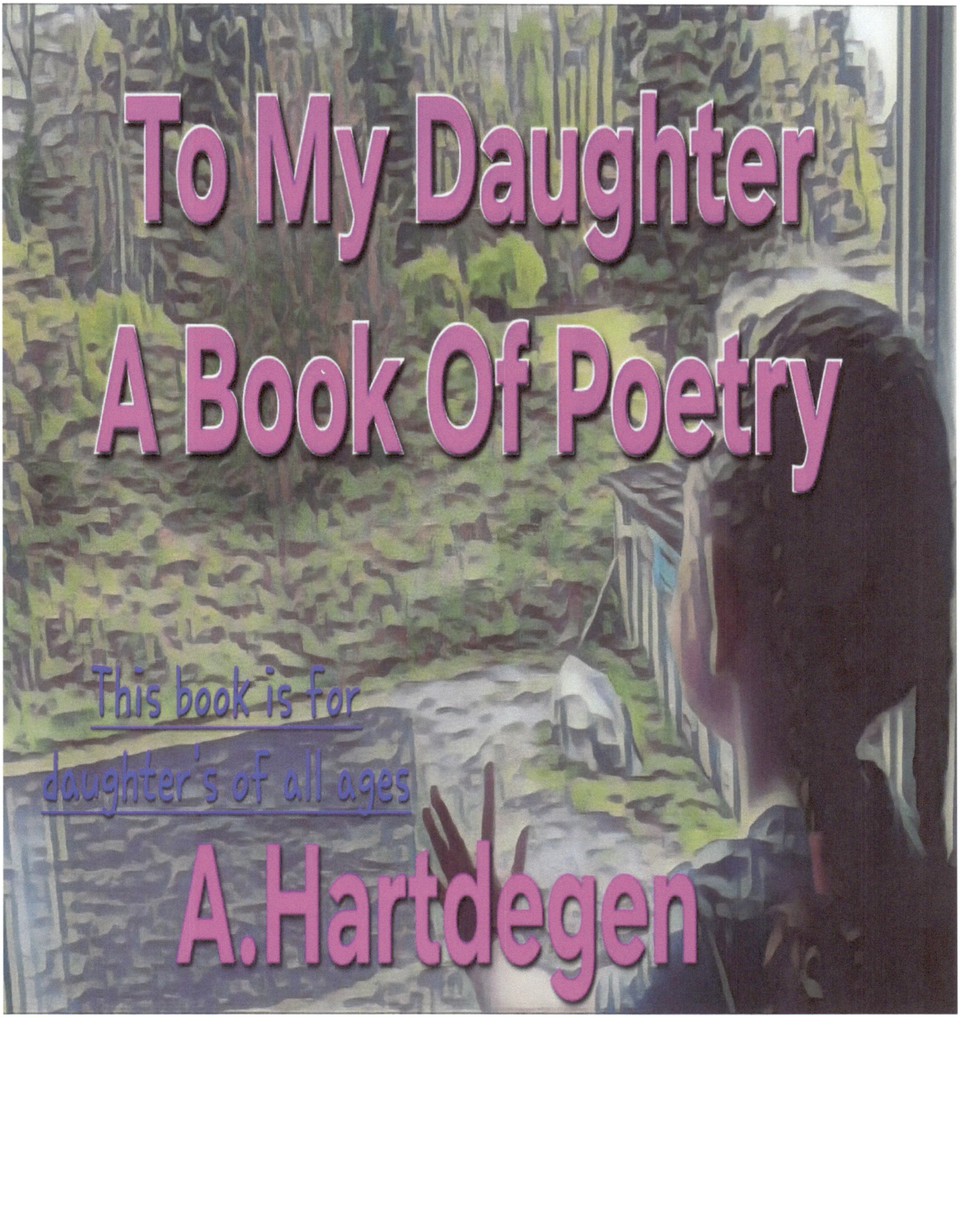

To My Daughter
A Book Of Poetry

This book is for daughter's of all ages

A.Hartdegen

To My Daughter A Book Of Poetry

By A.Hartdegen

ISBN 9798995160649

Publishing A.Hartdegen

To My Daughter: A Book of Poetry

This book is a timeless collection of 29 heartfelt poems celebrating the love, joy, and wonder between a parent and child. This book is for daughters of all ages from little girls to grown women and makes a cherished gift for birthdays, holidays, or simply to remind your daughter, she is loved, valued, and always held close to your heart.

Table of Contents

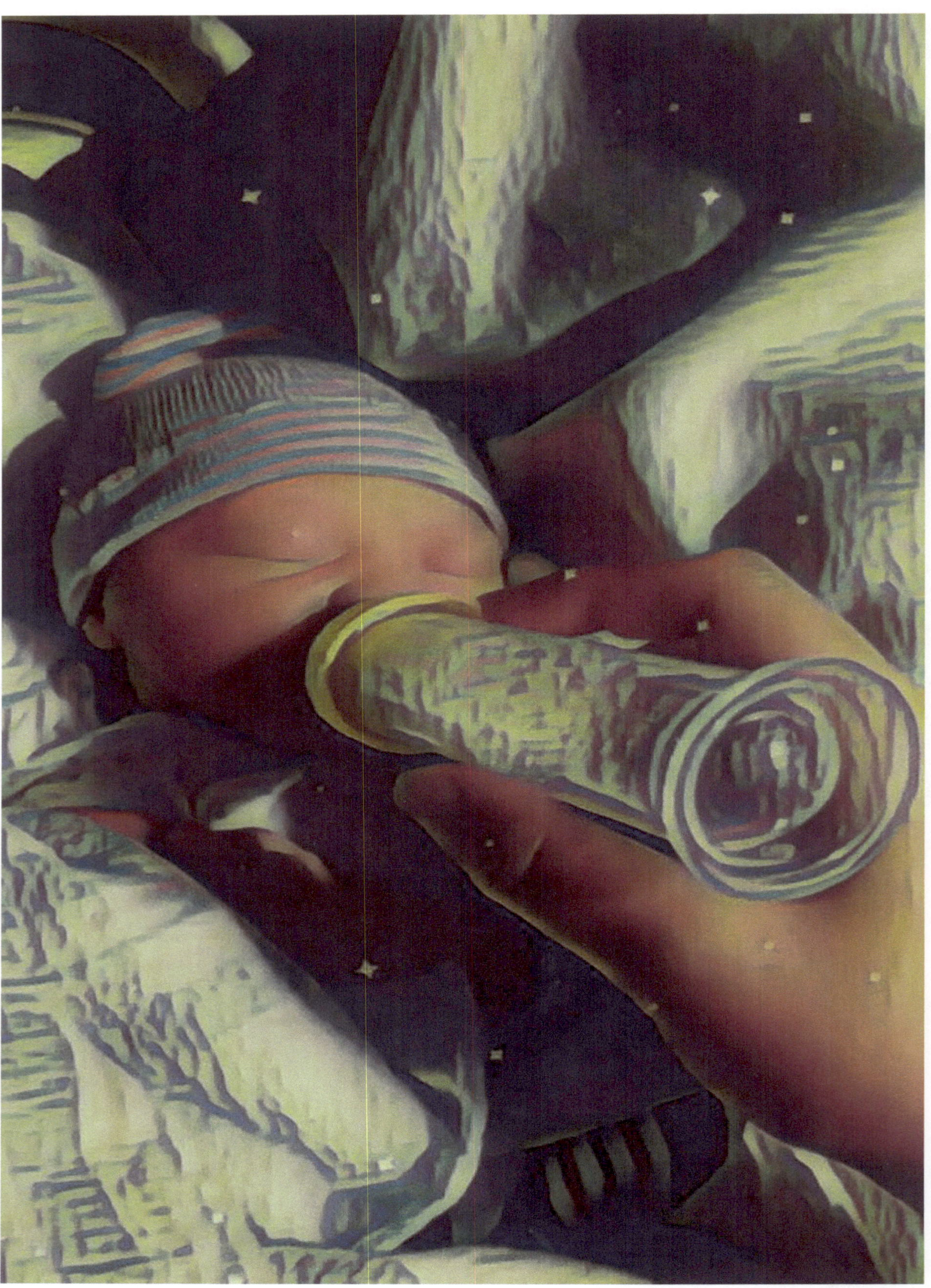

You Are My Miracle

The moment you came, my world was new,
The sky held light it never knew.
Your tiny cry, your fragile hands,
Redrew my heart, rewrite its plans.

I dreamed of love, but not like this,
A living soul, a breath, a kiss.
You showed me strength I couldn't see,
You built the better part of me.

Not chance, not luck, nor fleeting art,
You are the pulse within my heart.
A miracle both strong and true,
The world feels brighter loving you

I
BRIGHTEN
MOMMY'S
DAY

The Day the World Changed

The stars leaned close, the skies grew wide,
The moment you were by my side.
The air stood still, the earth took pause,
As if it knew the grandest cause.

Your eyes were lanterns, soft and new,
They lit my soul, they split me through.
A single breath, a tender sound,
And heaven's chorus gathered 'round.

No clock could tick, no sun could shine,
The day you came, the world was mine.
A shift so vast, yet clear, yet true—
The day it changed... was the day of you.

I Found Forever in You

I thought forever lived in time,
In stars that burn, in bells that chime.
But then you breathed, and then I knew,
Forever's face was carved in you.

Not in the sun that learns to fade,
Not in the plans the future made.
It isn't found in stone or flame,
Forever answers to your name.

For love like this will never cease,
It bends but holds, it breaks to peace.
Through every loss, through all I do,
I found forever
in loving you.

Made of Stardust

They say the stars are far away,
Too high to touch, too bright to stay.
But when I held you, small and new,
I saw the galaxies in you.

Your laughter shines, your spirit glows,
A secret every parent knows.
That in your skin, so soft, so fair,
The dust of stars is resting there.

Your tiny hands could shape the sky,
Could hold the moon, could make it sigh.
Each breath you take, a comet's flight,
Each heartbeat sparks eternal light.

You are not small, though you are young,
You hold the skies from which we're sprung.
A universe, both wild and true—
The cosmos dreamed and gifted you.

And as you grow, may you always see,
The magic flowing endlessly.
For in your eyes, the worlds reside,
The endless wonder where stars collide.

Muddy Shoes, Sparkling Eyes

Muddy shoes and sparkling eyes,
A world of wonder in your size.
You chase the wind, you jump, you run,
Each day a story, each day new sun.

Your giggles echo, pure delight,
From morning's glow to fading night.
The puddles splash beneath your feet,
The world becomes a playground sweet.

Grass-stained knees and hair askew,
Each mess a masterpiece, made by you.
The simple moments, wild and true,
Are painted bright in every hue.

And when you look my way and smile,
The earth itself could pause awhile.
For in those eyes, so full, so wise,
I see the magic that never dies.

Bedtime Negotiator

The clock ticks on, the stars appear,
Yet you declare, "I'm not sleepy, dear!"
You bargain, plead, you twist and sway,
A tiny diplomat at end of day.

One more story, a drink, a hug,
You tug the covers, and give a shrug.
Your eyes wide open, schemes in tow,
The master of "just one more thing," I know.

I watch you fight the gentle night,
As melatonin starts its quiet fight.
Your yawns arrive, but you resist,
With clever words and cheeky twist.

I laugh and sigh, I play the game,
Each night the rules are never the same.
Yet in these moments, soft and true,
I find more love than I ever knew.

So run your talks, your witty ways,
And fill the nights with playful days.
For one day soon, you'll drift alone,
But now these negotiations are all our own.

Your Silly Questions

"Why is the sky so blue?" you ask,
"Do clouds get tired of their task?"
Each question tumbles, wild and free,
A river of wonder flowing from thee.

"Can cats talk?" you wonder aloud,
"Do stars hide beneath their cloud?"
Your mind, a garden, endless, bright,
Blooming with questions from morning to night.

I try to answer, I try to guide,
But mostly I just sit beside
The miracle of your curious mind,
The endless "whys" you leave behind.

Each silly question, small and sweet,
Turns ordinary moments into treats.
And in your eyes, so wide, so true,
I see the world again, thanks to you

Dancing in the Kitchen

Barefoot spins on the tiled floor,
Giggles echo from wall to door.
We twirl, we leap, we spin around,
Our laughter leaps without a sound.

Music bursts from our hearts so bright,
Morning, evening, or fading light.
Little feet that stomp and glide,
Hands held tight, joy amplified.

Flailing arms and wild hair,
Crazy moves without a care.
The world outside can wait its turn,
Inside this room, our hearts still burn.

And when the dancing comes to end,
I hold these memories, my dearest friend.
For in each twirl, each joyful spin,
I find the light that lives within.

Winter
Wonderland

The World Through Your Eyes

The world is bigger when I see
Its colors dancing inside of thee.
Each flower blooms, each cloud drifts by,
A magic hidden in your sigh.

The simplest things become brand new,
A puddle's ripple, a sky so blue.
The wind can whisper, the trees can sing,
And every small sound a joy can bring.

Your wonder turns the mundane bright,
Transforms the shadows into light.
I watch, amazed, as you explore,
And find the beauty I'd ignored before.

Through your eyes, the world expands,
A universe held within your hands.
And in that gaze, so soft, so true,
I fall in love with life anew.

Stronger Than You Know

You run through life with fearless eyes,
A world of wonder in your skies.
Each stumble, fall, each little tear,
Is proof you're brave beyond your years.

The wind may push, the rain may fall,
But you will rise and stand through all.
Your laughter shields, your courage shows,
You're stronger than the world yet knows.

Each tiny step, each daring try,
Is firework sparks against the sky.
And when I watch, my heart will swell,
For in your strength, my soul can dwell.

No matter what the days may bring,
You're made to dance, to fly, to sing.
So take the world, let courage flow,
Remember always — stronger than you know.

Choosing Kindness

A helping hand, a gentle glance,
You turn the smallest acts to dance.
A laugh you share, a hug you give,
In your bright world, the world can live.

You hold a door, you share your toy,
Each little act ignites pure joy.
No cape required, no grand parade,
Just love in motion, quietly made.

I watch you shine in ways unseen,
A tiny heart, so bold, so keen.
And in these moments, soft and small,
I see the wonder that conquers all.

The world may roar, the days may spin,
But kindness grows where you begin.
So choose it freely, let it flow,
And know how much your light will show.

14

Courage in the Quiet

You try new things, you take small steps,
You face the day with tiny breaths.
The world is big, but still you grow,
Learning all the things you need to know.

And every little thing you do
Fills my heart with love, through and through.

My darling child, my soul's own song,
I love you more than words belong.
And in your quiet, fearless ways,
You teach me love for all my days.

The Sound of Your Laughter

The sound of your laughter fills the air,
A melody light beyond compare.
It dances through hallways, soft and free,
A song that belongs to only me.

It bubbles like rivers, it sparkles like rain,
It chases away even the deepest pain.
A giggle, a chuckle, a joyous squeal,
A sound so alive, it teaches me to feel.

No treasure on Earth, no gem or gold,
Could match the delight that you unfold.
A laugh so bright, a voice so true,
The world is richer for the sound of you.

And when you laugh, the stars take note,
The trees bend low, the rivers float.
All creation pauses just to hear,
Your laughter, when it's coming near!

Storms Will Pass

The clouds may gather, dark and wide,
The waves may crash, the winds may hide.
But even when the shadows stay,
The morning sun will find its way.

Life may shake and make you fall,
But love will lift you through it all.
No storm can steal, no night can last,
The fiercest winds will fade at last.

And when you're lost, when skies turn gray,
I'll hold your hand and help you stay.
For every storm you'll ever face,
My love will be your safest place.

So trust, my child, when dark skies mass,
The light returns. The storms will pass.

Dream Big, Little One

Dream big, my child, the stars are near,
They shine to guide, to calm your fear.
The sky is wide, the world is vast,
But love will hold you firm and fast.

Build castles high upon the sand,
Reach for horizons, take a stand.
No dream's too far, no wish too small,
You have the strength to chase them all.

And if the world feels much too wide,
Remember I am by your side.
Through twists and turns, through loss or gain,
My love will steady you through pain.

So dream, my darling, chase the skies,
With wonder glowing in your eyes.
For in your heart, a light shines true.
There's nothing you cannot pursue.

Little Hands, Big Heart

Your little hands make quite a mess,
With finger paints and sticky dress.
They grab the cookies, sneak a bite,
They hold on tight with all their might.

They build tall towers, knock them down,
They drum on tables, dance around.
They splash in puddles, clap with cheer,
And tug my sleeve to pull me near.

They wave hello, they wave goodbye,
They point at every bird that flies.
So tiny, yet they do their part—
Such little hands, such a big heart.

Forever your Home

I've watched you grow, year after year,
Each step you take, I hold so dear.
From tiny hands to dreams so wide,
You bloom with wonder by my side.

The little girl I used to know
Now shines with grace, begins to grow.
A young woman, strong and true,
The world feels brighter seeing you.

Yet as you change, one thing will stay—
My love will never drift away.
Through every season, time, or place,
You'll always find my warm embrace.

So chase your dreams, the skies, the sea—
Forever your home will live in me.

Magic in the Ordinary

The smallest things can light the day—
A blooming flower, a child at play.
The quiet hum of passing time,
Becomes a song, becomes a rhyme.

I see the world made new through you,
In every shade, in every hue.
The way you pause, the way you stare,
At fleeting moments, unaware.

A firework sky, a first snowfall,
A pumpkin glowing in the hall.
Each wonder feels like it's brand new,
Because I get to see it with you.

Your shining eyes, your eager grin,
Remind me where the joy begins.
Through you I learn, through you I see,
The world is full of mystery.

The Gift of Time

From an ultrasound heartbeat to seeing a tiny hand.
A spark of life I could barely understand.
Each breath you took, each blink, each sigh,
Was a universe unfolding before my eyes.

I watched your first laugh light up the room,
A burst of sunshine that chased away gloom.
Your curiosity, wild and bright,
Turned ordinary moments into pure delight.

And every day I marveled anew,
At the magic of simply being with you.
The hours slipped by, like rivers that run,
Each one a treasure beneath the sun.

Time is the gift, both fleeting and true,
Each moment a treasure I hold of you.
Though seasons change and years may climb,
I'll love you forever, beyond all time.

Eyes Like Windows

Your eyes are windows, clear and bright,
Opening wide to the world's delight.
I see the sunrise, the storms, the skies,
Reflected softly where wonder lies.

Through them I glimpse your endless dreams,
Your laughter rippling like gentle streams.
The smallest things become so grand,
When seen through eyes that understand.

They hold the questions you haven't asked,
The quiet bravery in each small task.
And in their depths, I often find,
The purest love of humankind.

So let your gaze forever roam,
For in your eyes, I see my home.

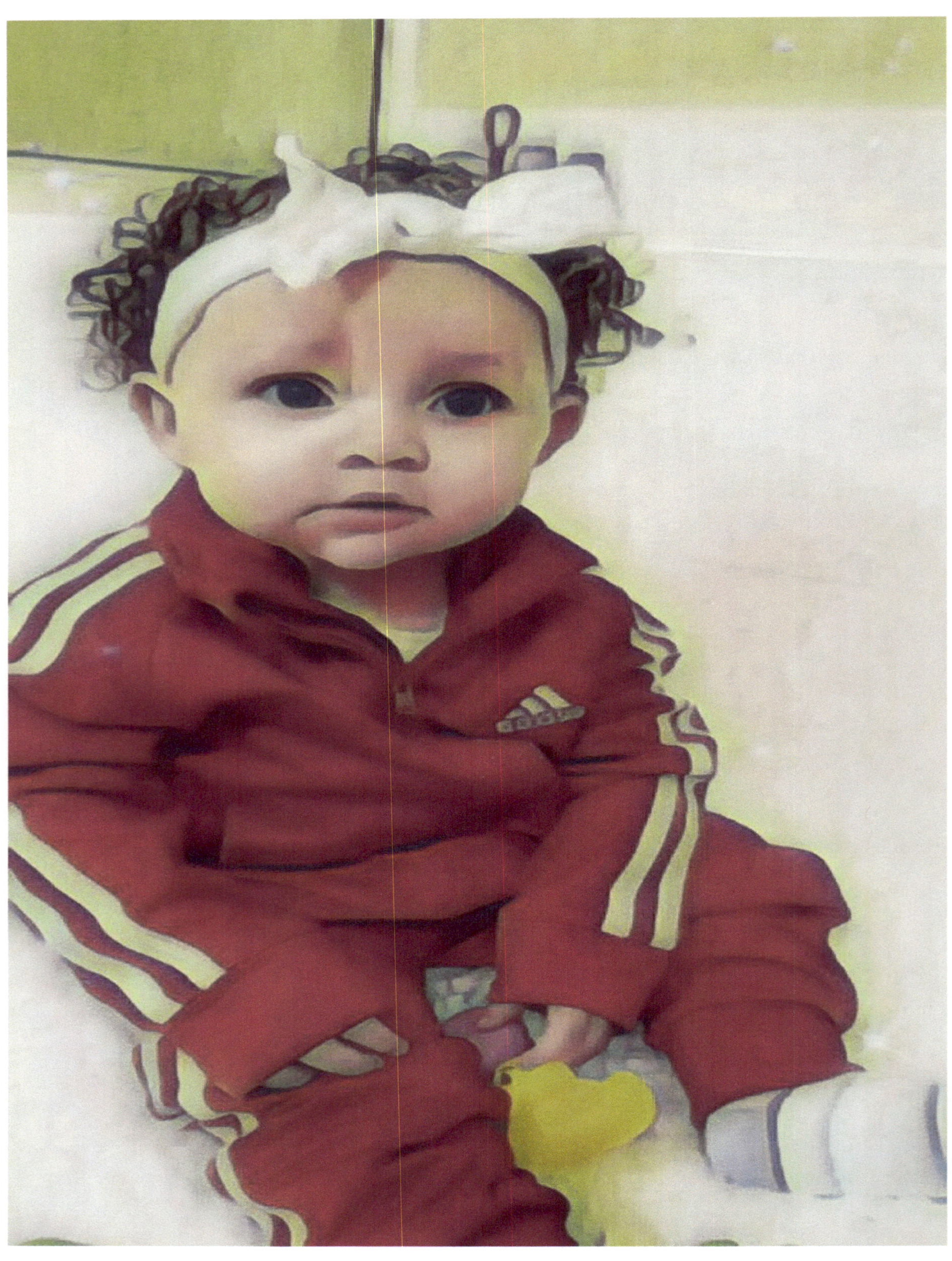

A World to Explore

You've grown into the woman you were meant to be,
With dreams as wide as the endless sea.
The choices now are yours to make,
Each path a story only you can take.

Responsibility walks beside your stride,
As I remain a faithful friend, a trusted guide.
Freedom calls with a gentle tone,
To build a life, and a place your own.

One day you'll laugh in a home you fill,
With children's joy and voices shrill.
A family born of love so true,
A mirror of the heart I see in you.

So step into the world with courage and grace,
With wisdom written upon your face.
And know that though your journey soars,
You carry my love forevermore.

Firsts You'll Remember

The first time you crawled across the floor,
The first time you opened a brand-new door.
Your first laugh, your first big cry,
The first time you reached for the sky.

The first ice cream that dripped on your chin,
The first time you raced the wind with a grin.
The first scraped knee, the first tight hug,
The first time you ran through rain so smug.

Every first, a memory spun,
A tiny spark, a rising sun.
Each one a treasure, bright and true,
Forever a part of me and you.

So hold them close, each joy, each start,
The little firsts that shape the heart.
For all the firsts you'll ever do,
The world became more magic with you.

Lessons Along the Way

Walk softly through the crowded streets,
Listen to hearts, not just their beats.
Kindness is a light that never fades,
Even when the world casts darker shades.

Stand tall when storms begin to rage,
Let patience guide you through each stage.
Speak your truth, but temper it with care,
For wisdom lives where love is shared.

Choose your friends as stars in the night,
Shining with honesty, blazing with light.
Let laughter be your constant friend,
And hold your spirit strong to the end.

Remember, my child, as you grow and strive,
The world is tough, yet full of life.
Carry these lessons, let them stay,
And let your heart lead you on your way.

Threads of You

Every morning, every night,
I see your soul, your spark, your light.
From tiny fingers to hopeful eyes,
You've stitched your dreams across my skies.

Each tear you've shed, each laugh you've shared,
Every scraped knee, each time I've cared,
Has woven threads of love so true,
A warm and safe quilt made by you.

The world I knew is not the same,
It shifts and changes, calls your name.
Yet through the storms, the things you try,
You grow a heart both brave and high.

So sleep, my darling, snuggled tight,
Wrapped in love through every night.
Each thread is proof, in all you do,
I hope you know I'm proud of you.

Fire in Your Soul

There's a fire in your soul, a light in your eyes,
A spark that will carry you high to the skies.
No storm can break you, no shadow can stay,
Your spirit was born to brighten the way.

When the world feels heavy, and trials are near,
Remember my voice, remember I'm here.
Strength isn't loud, it's steady and true,
And every flame burning was planted in you.

Dream without limits, stand strong, be bold,
Your story's worth more than silver or gold.
Through every challenge, through each new role,
The world is brighter from the fire in your soul.

Seasons of You

Spring was your laughter, your curious start,
Tiny hands reaching, a wide-open heart.
The world was new, each color so bright,
Everyday blooming with pure delight.

Summer was sunshine, bold and free,
Running through life with wild energy.
Dreams like fireflies lit up the night,
Hope in your step, your spirit alight.

Autumn will come with wisdom and grace,
Strength in your voice, peace on your face.
Lessons will gather like leaves that fall,
Teaching you gently the worth of it all.

And winter will bring a quiet hue,
But beauty will shine in all that you do.
Through every season, one thing stays true:
I'll always be proud of the seasons of you.

Forever My Little Girl

I held you first, so small, so new,
The world felt brighter because of you.
Your tiny fingers, your gentle curl,
You'll always be my little girl.

I watched you grow with wonder each day,
Finding your voice, your laughter, your way.
The years flew by in a tender swirl,
Yet still, you're forever my little girl.

One day you'll walk with strength and pride,
A family, a life, all there by your side.
But no matter how far your dreams may unfurl,
You'll always be my little girl.

And when I'm old and the nights are long,
I'll hear your heart in a familiar song.
Through time, through change, through all of this world,
You'll always, forever, be my little girl.

Small Hands, Big Universe

Within my palm, a hand so small—
Yet greater than the stars that fall.
The galaxies could fade, grow dim…
The cosmos rests where love begins.

Through endless void, through vast abyss,
No truth compares to this, to this.
A fleeting spark, a fragile start,
The cosmos beats within my heart.

These tiny fingers curl, command,
More gravity than time can stand.
They chart the skies, they bend the years…
The cosmos whispers through my tears.

And when the starlight fades from every view,
The only universe that matters is the one with you.

For the Love of My Daughter

From the moment you came, my world was remade,
A light in the darkness, a love that won't fade.
Through laughter and tears, through journeys we've known,
You've taught me the meaning of love fully grown.

Your footsteps may wander, your dreams may ascend,
Through twists in the road, around every bend.
But wherever you go, whatever you do,
My heart walks beside every part of you.

For the love of my daughter is endless, untamed,
A fire, a promise, a soul unchained.
It carries through seasons, through time, through skies,
A bond everlasting that never dies.

So take this with you, wherever you roam,
The love of your parent will guide you home.
A gift unbroken, steadfast, and true—
Forever, my daughter, I believe in you.

To My Daughter A Book Of Poetry

Inspired by the love for my daughter, Winter, this book was born from the deepest corners of a parent's heart.

To My Daughter A Book of Poetry is a collection of timeless poems celebrating the unbreakable bond between parent and child. Each poem captures the magic, wonder, laughter, and tears that come with watching a daughter grow — from her very first steps to the milestones of adulthood.

This book is written not just for my daughter, but for daughters everywhere. Whether gifted on a birthday, holiday, or simply as a reminder, these words speak the truth every daughter deserves to hear: You are cherished. You are loved. We are proud of you. And we will always want the very best for you.

A keepsake for all ages, this collection is a heartfelt tribute from every parent to every daughter — a reminder that the love between parent and child is forever.

www.ingramcontent.com/pod-product-compliance
Lightning Source LLC
LaVergne TN
LVHW070147110826
845147LV00002B/339
* 9 7 9 8 9 9 5 1 6 0 6 4 9 *